KV-031-389

Baby

AND

Toddler

~ TREASURY ~

Introduction

From my experience as a mother and a Nursery Nurse, I know that there is great satisfaction in discovering a new book for your child that can be used time and time again. The *Baby and Toddler Treasury* will, I feel, be one such book to enjoy together – popular with you as well as your children!

There is an enormously wide range of activities and ideas included in the book – suitable for "activity times" when you can't get out and about for whatever reason, and for "snuggle-down-together times".

Play is vital for all babies and toddlers, and the educational dimension of play has long been recognised. The beautifully detailed illustrations in this *Treasury* offer many ways to learn through play.

The clear, bright "Alphabet animal" pages give a lovely opportunity to practise first letter sounds, making recognition fun. The "Make and play" pages help to develop fine motor control and creative skills.

Taken as a whole, this nursery collection provides ample practice for all your child's early learning skills.

Have fun!

Jo Thomas, NNEB

Baby
AND
Toddler

~ TREASURY ~

Written by Nicola Baxter and Marie Birkinshaw
Illustrated by Frank Endersby

ARMADILLO

This edition is published by Armadillo, an imprint of Anness Publishing Ltd,
Hermes House, 88–89 Blackfriars Road, London SE1 8HA;
tel. 020 7401 2077; fax 020 7633 9499

www.annesspublishing.com

Anness Publishing has a new picture agency outlet for images for publishing, promotions or
advertising. Please visit our website www.practicalpictures.com for more information.

Produced for Anness Publishing Ltd by Nicola Baxter

Editorial consultant: Ronne Randall
Designer: Amanda Hawkes
Production designer: Amy Barton

ETHICAL TRADING POLICY

Because of our ongoing ecological investment programme, you, as our customer, can have the
pleasure and reassurance of knowing that a tree is being cultivated on your behalf to naturally
replace the materials used to make the book you are holding. For further information about
this scheme, go to www.annesspublishing.com/trees

PUBLISHER'S NOTE

Although the advice and information in this book are believed to be accurate and true at the
time of going to press, neither the authors nor the publisher can accept any legal responsibility
or liability for any errors or omissions that may be made.

Contents

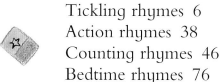

Tickling rhymes!

Round and round the garden

Round and round the garden
Like a teddy bear,
One step,
Two steps,
Tickle you under there!

Pat-a-cake

Pat-a-cake! Pat-a-cake! Baker's man,
Bake me a cake as fast as you can.
Pat it and prick it and mark it with B,
And put it in the oven for Baby and me!

This little piggy

This little piggy went to market.

This little piggy stayed at home.

This little piggy had roast beef.

This little piggy had none.

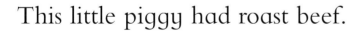

And this little piggy cried *wee, wee, wee*
All the way home!

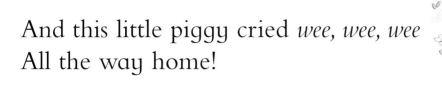

The Ugly Duckling

Mother Duck

ducklings

ugly duckling

lake

reeds

watched as five fluffy hatched from the eggs in her nest. Then waited for the last egg to hatch. At last, the egg cracked. Out came a very ! The other laughed at him.

showed the how to swim on the cool, blue . But the just hid in the , because the other laughed at him.

led her little ones into the . But the hid behind the straw, because the other laughed at him.

The  was so sad that he ran away. All through winter he stayed away from the big  . When spring came, the  saw some white birds flying in the  .

barn

sky

One swan called to the  . "How beautiful you are!" he said. "Come and join us!"

swan

The  looked at himself in the water. He wasn't an  any more! He was a beautiful  !

And the  never laughed at him again.

Another you!

You will need:

mirror

roll of old wallpaper

pencil

red, yellow, blue and
white poster paints

wool the same colour
as your hair

PVA glue

paintbrush

baking tray

Ask a grown-up to help you make
this very familiar person!

1 Roll the wallpaper out flat on
the floor.

2 Lie down on the wallpaper and ask
your helper to draw around you.

You can mix all
the colours you
need from four
pots of paint.

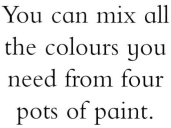

red + yellow =
orange

blue + yellow =
green

3 Look in the
mirror. What
colours are
your eyes,
hair, skin
and clothes?

red + blue = purple

4 Now decorate the
wallpaper person to
look just like you. Stick
on wool to make hair.

red + blue + yellow =
brown

5 Pour paint into the
baking tray and make
foot and hand prints on
a separate piece of paper.
When they are dry, cut
them out and stick them
on your person.

red + white = pink
Mix brown, pink,
white and yellow
for skin colours.

Picnic mix-up

Giraffe is last to arrive for a picnic in the park. Use your finger to help him find the way and collect up all the food that his friends have dropped.

Giraffe has lots of friends!
What are they all doing?

Noisy farmyard

calf

foal

piglet

lamb

duckling

chick

What are these noisy animals saying in the farmyard?

Neigh!

Baa!

Can you match the mothers and babies at the side of the picture?

cow

horse

pig

sheep

duck

hen

Pp Pp Pp Pp Pp

pencil

Percy Panda has painted
a picture.

polar
bear

penguin

pan

pear

pixie

pumpkin

What else begins with **p**?

pen

paper

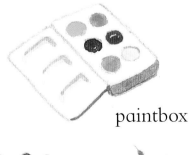
paintbox

present

pond

parrot

puzzle

Cc Cc Cc Cc Cc

cow

camera

crab

Carrie Camel has come to a coconut.

What else begins with **c**?

clown

castle

car

cabbage

clock

C

carrot

candle

calendar

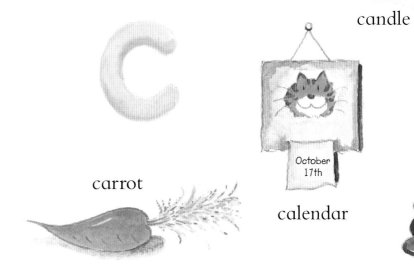

cake

Chicken Licken

Chicken Licken

king

Henny Penny

Goosey Loosey

Turkey Lurkey

One day  was coming out of her house when OUCH! something fell on her head. "Oh, no! The sky is falling down!" said  . "I must go and tell the  !"

On the way,  met and  . "The sky is falling down, and I'm going to tell the ," said  . "Please come too!"

So  , and  went on their way until they met  . "The sky is falling down, and I'm going to tell the ," said  . "Please come too!"

So , and went on their way. But someone was listening. It was ! "I'll pretend to be the !" he said. And he put a royal sign upon his .

Soon , and arrived. They knocked at the and saw… ! Quickly, they slammed the and ran all the way back to 's house. On the ground was an .

"I think this is what hit you," said . "We don't need to tell the after all!"

Foxy Loxy

door

acorn

Gg Gg Gg Gg Gg

Gary Goat has grown
some green grapes.

gate

glue

grass

grain

grasshopper

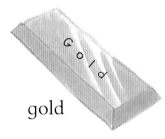

gold

guitar

What else begins with **g**?

garden

g

grapes

glider

glass

Rr Rr Rr Rr Rr

robot

Rosie Rabbit races
down the river.

ruler

ribbon

ring

rain

rainbow

river

raccoon

What else begins with **r**?

rocket

rocking horse

rhinoceros

raspberry

roof

At the seaside

Can you find all the little pictures
in the big picture?

sandcastle

sun

iced lolly

bucket and spade

waves

beach ball

How many different colours
can you see at the seaside?

crab

deckchair

seaweed

beach umbrella

starfish

yacht

Rainbow colours

Help the rainbow-makers find their way over the mountains to their rainbow machine. Make sure you pass all the colours they need to make a rainbow.

What else can you see in the picture?

Funny clown face

You will need:

large plate

scissors

wool or string

card

elastic (not too thin)

PVA glue

pencil

paint and brush

Ask a grown-up to help you make this marvellous mask!

1 Draw around the plate on to some card.

2 Draw some hair, a hat and a tie on to the circle.

3 Ask your grown-up helper to cut around the face and make holes for your eyes.

4 Stick on wool or string for hair.

5 Stick on a large red cardboard nose.

6 Make a red banana shape
for a mouth, with string
lips in the middle.

7 Decorate the
rest of the face,
hat and tie
with paints or
pieces of card.
The clown
faces on
these pages
will give you
some ideas.

8 Ask your
helper to make
a hole either side
of the mask and
knot the elastic
through. Check it is
not too tight.

9 Have fun being a clown!

Can you do
some funny
clown tricks?

Do a wobbly
clown's walk.

Make silly
clown noises.

Try to juggle
some beanbags.

Ww Ww Ww Ww

Wanda Whale washes the windows with waves.

windmill

wheel

What else begins with **w**?

wolf

well

waterfall

watch

wallet

web

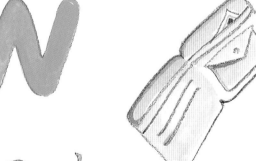

wheelbarrow

whistle

Ll Ll Ll Ll Ll Ll

Lucy Lion has lost her lizard.

lamb

ladybird

leaf

luggage

lemon

What else begins with **l**?

lightning

lawnmower

label

ladder

lunchbox

leopard

Shopping

Can you find all the little pictures in the big picture?

oranges

cheese

tomatoes

milk

juice

bread

What do you like to
buy when you go shopping?

wire basket

trolley

till

money

bag

receipt

Aa Aa Aa Aa Aa

artist

acrobat

armchair

aeroplane

Andy Ant is an angry
ant on an acorn.

What else begins with **a**?

a

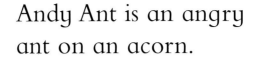

apple

astronaut

anchor

ambulance

actor

Ff Ff Ff Ff Ff Ff

Fiona is a friendly fish.

frog

fireworks

fountain

flowers

Farm

farm

fire

flamingo

What else begins with **f**?

flag

footprint

f

feather

fish

flour

fork

Three Little Pigs

pigs

straw

wolf

sticks

Once there were three little . The first little pig built a house of . But when the big bad came along, he huffed and he puffed and he blew the house down with a CRASH!

The second little pig built a house of . But when the big bad came along, he huffed and he puffed and he blew the house down with a CRUNCH!

The third little pig built a house

of  . But when the big bad

came along, he could not

blow the down!

He huffed and puffed and puffed and

huffed. But still the big bad

could not blow the down.

The was angry and climbed

down the . But the third little

pig was ready. He put a

under the . Then SPLASH!

That was the end of the

big bad !

bricks

house

chimney

cooking pot

Ii Ii Ii   Jj Jj Jj Jj

iron

igloo

invitation

ink

ice-cream

iceberg

Iggy Iguana is itching and
Julia Jellyfish is jiggling.

What else begins with **i** or **j**?

Jeep

juice

juggler

jigsaw
puzzle

jewellery

Kk Kk Kk Kk

kissing

key

kicking

Kelly Koala keeps kittens in the kitchen.

What else begins with **k**?

king

kite

kangaroo

keyhole

kitten

kiwi

Action rhymes

The wheels on the bus

The wheels on the bus go round and round,
Round and round, round and round,
The wheels on the bus go round and round,
All day long.

The wipers on the bus go swish, swish, swish,
Swish, swish, swish, swish, swish, swish,
The wipers on the bus go swish, swish, swish,
All day long.

The bell on the bus goes ding, ding, ding,
Ding, ding, ding, ding, ding, ding,
The bell on the bus goes ding, ding, ding,
All day long.

The children on the bus bounce up and down,
Up and down, up and down,
The children on the bus bounce up and down,
All day long.

Can you make up some more verses
about what happens on the bus?

The grand old Duke of York

Oh, the grand old Duke of York
He had ten thousand men;
He marched them up to the top
   of the hill,
And he marched them down again.

And when they were up, they were up,
And when they were down, they were down,
And when they were only halfway up,
They were neither up nor down.

Peter and Paul

Two little birds sat on
   a wall,
One named Peter,
One named Paul.
Fly away, Peter!
Fly away, Paul!
Come back, Peter!
Come back, Paul!

Jump and jiggle

Can you?

Can you wriggle 10 fingers and then jiggle 10 toes?

Can you do 9 jumps and then wiggle 1 nose?

Can you clap 8 times and then pat 2 knees?

Can you do 7 skips and then
SNEEZE SNEEZE SNEEZE?

Can you do 6 bends and
then 4 hops?

Now count to 5 and
then shout, "STOP!"

Chocolate crispies

You will need:

mixing bowl

spoon

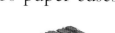

10 paper cases

100g cooking chocolate

50g crispy rice cereal

10ml (2 teaspoons)
golden syrup

5ml (1 tsp) hot water

5ml (1 tsp) margarine

25g chopped dried
apricots

Ask a grown-up to help you make
these yummy treats!

Wash your hands
and put on an
apron before
you start.

1 Ask your grown-up
helper to melt the
chocolate in a
microwave or over
hot water and
then mix in
the golden
syrup, hot
water and
margarine.

2 Put the crispy cereal in a mixing bowl and pour in the warm chocolate mixture. Stir quickly with a spoon until all the crispy cereal is covered with chocolate. Add the chopped apricots.

You could try these ingredients instead of the apricots:

raisins

cherries

marshmallows

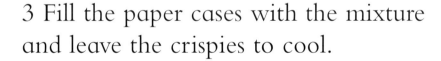

3 Fill the paper cases with the mixture and leave the crispies to cool.

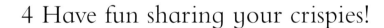

4 Have fun sharing your crispies!

chocolate drops

coloured chocolate sweets

Bb Bb Bb Bb Bb

ball

bed

bell

bubbles

bath

banana

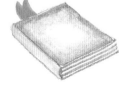

book

Billy Bear is batting
a ball.

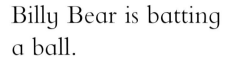

What else begins with **b**?

bee

bag

buttons

butterfly

bus

bicycle

bottle

building
bricks

boat

balloon

Mm Mm Mm

moon

monkey

magnet

Mary Mouse is making a mess.

What else begins with **m**?

mirror

mountain

motorcycle

mermaid

magician

m

money

milk

Counting Rhymes

One, two, three, four, five

One, two, three, four, five,
Once I caught a fish alive,
Six, seven, eight, nine, ten,
Then I let it go again.

Why did you let it go?
Because it bit my finger so!
Which finger did it bite?
This little finger on the right!

Baa, baa, black sheep

Baa, baa, black sheep,
Have you any wool?
Yes, sir, yes, sir,
Three bags full.
One for my master,
And one for my dame,
And one for the little boy
Who lives down the lane.

One, two, buckle my shoe

One, two, buckle my shoe;
Three, four, knock at the door;
Five, six, pick up sticks;
Seven, eight, lay them straight;
Nine, ten, my fat hen;
Eleven, twelve, dig and delve;
Thirteen, fourteen, maids a-courting;
Fifteen, sixteen, maids in the kitchen;
Seventeen, eighteen, maids in waiting;
Nineteen, twenty, my plate's empty.

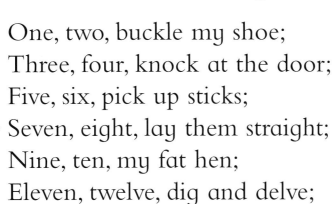

The Three Bears

cottage

porridge

Goldilocks

bowl

chair

It was breakfast time at the three bears'  . But the was too hot, so the bears went for a walk. Now, was also in the forest. She smelt the and went inside the .

tried the big and the medium . But the in the little tiny was just right. So she ate it all up!

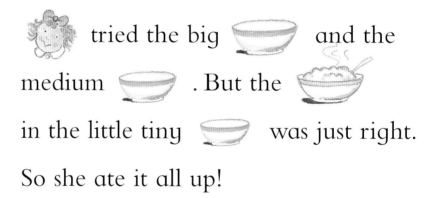

sat in the big and the medium . But the little tiny was just right … until it broke into pieces!

 went upstairs. She tried the big  and the medium . But the little tiny  was just right, and she fell fast asleep.

bed

The three bears came back to the . They saw the . They saw the . They saw . They saw the . They saw .

bowls

chairs

Suddenly the little girl woke up and saw the three bears. Quickly she ran out of the  and was never seen again.

beds

Ee Ee Ee Ee Ee

Elsie Elephant is eating an enormous egg.

eagle

escalator

ears

eggs

envelope

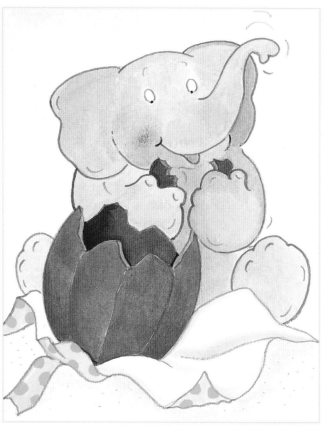

What else begins with **e**?

e

elephant

entrance

exit

explorer

Hh Hh Hh Hh

helicopter

hand

house

Hugo Hippo is still
hugely hungry.

What else begins with **h**?

hat

hammer

hospital

helmet

hill   hair

happy

h

heart

horse

A royal crown

You will need:

card

pencil and ruler

crayons and paints

scissors

PVA glue

sticky tape or staples

decorations

Ask a grown-up to help you make this lovely crown!

Follow the patterns below with your finger. Which one will you choose?

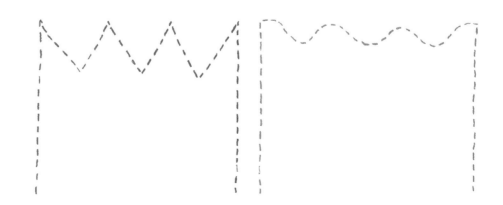

1 Ask your grown-up helper to cut a piece of card at least 20cm deep and long enough to go around your head.

2 Show your helper what kind of pattern you would like along the top. Help to draw it so the grown-up can cut it out.

3 Decorate your crown. You could use paints or crayons, then stick on any decorations you like.

4 When the glue is dry, help to bend the crown round and fix it with sticky tape or staples.

5 Enjoy being a King, Queen, Princess or Prince!

Wear your crown to sing some royal rhymes. Do you know these ones?

The Queen of Hearts

Old King Cole

Pussy Cat, Pussy Cat

Finger wiggles

Clench your fist to make a beehive.

Peep into your pretend beehive.

Gently unfold one finger at a time, pretending to make the bees fly away!

The busy beehive

Here is the busy beehive.
Where are the busy bees?

Hidden away where nobody sees.
Soon they come creeping out of the hive.

One…
       Two…
           Three…
              Four…
                  Five…

BUZZ! BUZZ! BUZZ! BUZZ! BUZZ!

Five little soldiers

Five little soldiers standing in a row.
Three are standing straight.
And two stand so.

Along comes the Captain,
And what do you think?

Up

jump the soldiers, quick as a wink!

Stand the fingers and thumb of one hand up in a line like soldiers.

Bend two fingers as if they are asleep.

March the thumb of your other hand across to the "soldier" fingers.

All five "soldier" fingers stand to attention.

Ss Ss Ss Ss Ss Ss

star

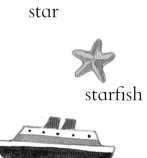

starfish

ship

stairs

Sally Snake is sipping
her savoury soup.

snail

seagull

spaghetti

swan

What else begins with **s**?

submarine

stamp

shell

scissors

spider

spaceship

Dd Dd Dd Dd Dd

dragon

Dora Duck is dipping
deep down.

dog

desert

door

digger

doctor

What else begins with **d**?

dinosaur

drum

d

dice

dentist

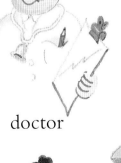
dancer

drawing

In the woods

Use your finger to follow the path through the woods. Can you name the woodland creatures that you meet along the way? What else can you see?

Xx Xx Xx Xx

Foxy Loxy plays the xylophone.

mixing

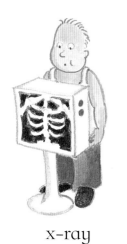

x-ray

ox

six

fox

taxi

What else has an **x** sound?

boxes

exit

Yy Yy   Zz Zz

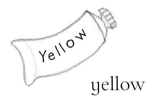
yellow

Yakkety Yak yawns as Zippy Zebra zooms around the zoo.

zebra

zero

yo yo

yolk

What else begins with **y** or **z**?

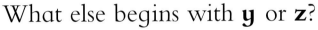

yawn

yogurt

zip

zigzag

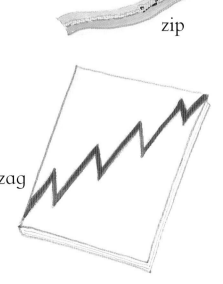

Three Billy Goats

grass

river

bridge

greedy troll

the little
billy goat

The Three Billy Goats Gruff wanted to eat the 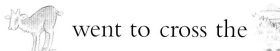 on the other side of the . But a guarded the only .

went to cross the .

Trip, trap, trip, trap!

UP jumped the . "I'll eat you for my breakfast!" he roared. "Don't eat me!' said . "Eat . He's much fatter than I am." So the let him pass.

Then went to cross the .

Trip, trap, trip, trap!

UP jumped the . "I'll eat you for my breakfast!" he roared.

"Don't eat me!' said .

"Eat . He's much fatter than

I am." So the let him pass.

the second
billy goat

Then went to cross the 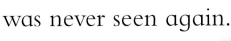 .

Trip, trap, trip, trap!

UP jumped the . "I'll eat

you for my breakfast!" he roared.

the third
billy goat

"Oh, no, you won't!" bellowed .

And he tossed over the

 and SPLASH! into the 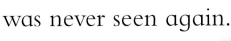 .

The was never seen again.

Oo Oo Oo Oo

Ozzie Ostrich has
opened an orange.

ostrich

oranges

oars

owl

office

oboe

What else begins with **o**?

oven

oil

octopus

table

trunk

telephone

turtle

tent

Tilly Tortoise has taken a taxi.

Taxi

What else begins with **t**?

t

towel

trumpet

train

toothpaste

toothbrush

tree

tiger

The Big Pancake

old lady

flour

pan

Big Pancake

door

One day an  decided to make some pancakes. She mixed some , some milk and an egg together, and poured the mixture into a hot .

At once she heard someone shouting, "I'm the , nice and hot! You won't catch me, no, certainly not!" The  leapt out of the  and on to the floor. It rolled right out of the .

"Stop!" cried the .

The  rolled and rolled. It rolled past a  and a  . But it didn't stop.

dog

The  rolled past a  and a  . But it didn't stop.

cat

horse

Then the  came to the place where 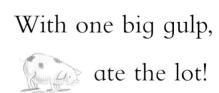 stood.  put out his snout and made the  trip. Then he tossed it and gave it a flip. "Mm, a  nice and not hot!"

cow

With one big gulp, 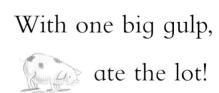 ate the lot!

Big Pig

Nn Nn Nn Nn

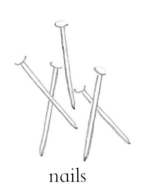

nails

night

necklace

Norman and the Newts
are noisy but nice.

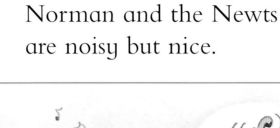

nurse

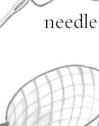

newspaper

What else begins with **n**?

n

needle

nest

net

Qq Qq Qq Qq Qq

queen

quilt

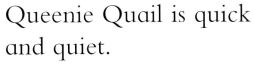
Queenie Quail is quick and quiet.

queue

Ssshhh!

Quiet!

What else begins with **qu**?

Quack!

quarter

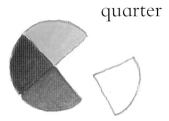

questions

On the move

Can you find all the little pictures
in the big picture?

car

van

lorry

tanker

bus

digger

What sounds do these vehicles make?

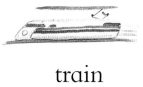

train

plane

narrow boat

motorbike

bicycle

hot-air balloon

Uu Uu Uu Uu

upside down

Uncle Umbrellabird is
upside down.

umbrella

up

undressing

unicorn

What else begins with **u**?

Oh no!

untidy

untied

under

Vv Vv Vv Vv Vv

Valerie Vole makes
vegetables vanish.

vulture

vacuum
cleaner

video
cassette

vase

What else begins with **v**?

volcano

violin

van

vegetables

Bedtime bear

It is Bubbly's bedtime, but all her night-time things are in the wrong place!

Follow the path through Bubbly's house to find everything she needs for a good night's sleep.

What do you like to have at bedtime?

Bedtime rhymes

Star song

Star light, star bright,
First star I see tonight,
I wish I may, I wish I might,
Have the wish I wish tonight.

Jack, be nimble

Jack, be nimble,
Jack, be quick,
Jack, jump over the candlestick!

How many miles to Babylon?

How many miles to Babylon?
Three score miles and ten.
Can I get there by candlelight?
Yes, and back again.
If your heels are nimble and light,
You may get there by candlelight.

Hush-a-bye, baby

Hush-a-bye, baby, on the treetop,
When the wind blows, the cradle will rock;
When the bough breaks, the cradle will fall,
Down will come baby, cradle and all.

Diddle, diddle, dumpling

Diddle, diddle, dumpling, my son John,
Went to bed with his trousers on!
One shoe off and one shoe on,
Diddle, diddle, dumpling, my son John.

Alphabet fun

a b c
d e f
g h i
j k l
m n o
p q r
s t u
v w x
y z

Look back through the book to find these pictures. What letter sound begins their names? Can you point to that letter?

Have fun singing the alphabet to the tune of *The Grand old Duke of York*, or another favourite nursery rhyme.

Number fun hunt

Go on a page-hunt to find:

1 The Ugly Duckling (page 8)

2 Bears on a see-saw (page 13)

3 Three Little Pigs (page 34)

4 Starfish (pages 22 and 23)

5 Hungry animals (pages 66 and 67)

6 Traffic cones (pages 70 and 71)

7 Rainbow colours (pages 24 and 25)

8 Butterflies (pages 58 and 59)

9 Rabbits (pages 40 and 41)

10 Funny clowns (pages 26 and 27)

Rhymes index

Can you remember these?